Rather than a series of revisions, Lita Hooper's elegant poems in *Thunder in Her Voice: The Narrative of Sojourner Truth* are striking illuminations that take us beyond the "facts" of Sojourner's life and into the "truth" of her thoughts, her fears, her hopes and her prayers. Hooper's genius lies in her capacity for empathy and her ability to write a poetic line of such simplicity and grace that it turns even the most harrowing facts into beautiful laments of pain and hope. This is a great way to encounter the humanity behind all historical narratives.

> —*Dr. Kwame S.N. Dawes*
> Louise Fry Scudder Professor of English
> Distinguished Poet in Residence
> Director of the South Carolina Poetry Initiative
> Director of the USC Arts Institute

Lita Hooper, in *Thunder in Her Voice*, breathes in Sojourner Truth's life and breathes out a testimony concerning the "inherited agony" that was slavery. Hooper's anointed poetry resonates with spirit-filled voices sounding a universal prayer for freedom and self-determination.

> —*Joanne Veal Gabbin*
> Furious Flower Poetry Center
> James Madison University

Thunder in Her Voice

The Narrative of Sojourner Truth

Willow Books, the Poetry Imprint of

AQUARIUS PRESS
Detroit, Michigan

Thunder in Her Voice
The Narrative of Sojourner Truth
Copyright © 2010 by Lita Hooper

Excerpts from Washington, M. , *Narrative of Sojourner Truth* (1993). New York: Vintage Books.

Cover Art: Krista Franklin with Stephen Flemister
Cover Design: Aquarius Press
Author Photo (back cover): Seth Ruff
ISBN 978-0-9819208-8-7
LCCN 2010922403

Willow Books, the Poetry Imprint of
AQUARIUS PRESS
PO Box 23096
Detroit, MI 48223
(877) 979-3639

Printed in the United States of America

These poems are responses to excerpts from the slave narrative of Sojourner Truth, one of America's most important civil rights activists. Each poem reflects the spirit of the men and women who resonate through Truth's biography.

Acknowledgments

This book was inspired by my lovely daughter, Sojourner Imani Simanga. My husband, Michael, and son, Malik, provided the motivation to complete the manuscript. Michael, director extraordinaire, made the first staged reading a success. Thank you for your creativity and love.

The Baobab Poetry Collective members were very helpful in providing feedback on many of the poems.

The City of Atlanta Office of Cultural Affairs awarded me an Emerging Artist Grant, which gave me the support needed to complete a handmade book and produce the first staged reading of these poems.

The final touches were made at the wonderful Soul Mountain Retreat, thanks to Marilyn Nelson.

My editor, Randall Horton, was incredibly patient and respectful of the work I presented. Heather Buchanan of Aquarius Press granted my wish for a "different" kind of book.

The immensely talented Krista Franklin made an original work of art for my cover. So talented!

Finally, the Cave Canem family, too many to name, gave me consistent support through numerous email, text, and Facebook messages.

Many thanks, Everyone!

Contents

Introduction

So many have told my story
sculpted my tenor easily
as pen stains the page.

But what I offer here is a life
of constant revision, God
my Greatest Editor!

Read this with open hearts
and you will come to know
not how I lived
but how to become glorious.

Women, slaves, all
take these poems: my offering.

Glory, glory! All around us
blessings unfolding.

*A*mong Isabella's earliest recollections was the
removal of her master, Charles Ardinburgh,
into his new house, which he had built for a hotel,
soon after the decease of his father. A cellar,
under this hotel, was assigned to his slaves, as
their sleeping apartment—all the slaves he
possessed, of both sexes, sleeping (as is quite
common in a state of slavery) in the same room
. . . She shudders, even now, as she goes back in
memory, and revisits this cellar. . .

Sleeping Quarters

Here misery unfolds   hovers
the way air weighs one down to sleep.
We lay in quiet gratitude
on thin wood and straw pallets
our breathing a testimony
to another day's survival.

Flanked by Bomefree and Mau-Mau
I hold a patient pose
as night's sound remind me
of life's abundance. I search

the darkened room
which is like the sky
spotted by the moon's mercy. Before
I close my eyes
I follow God's direction—
a silver streak breaking
through the panes
pointing.

*I*sabella's father was very tall and straight, when young, which gave him the name "Bomefree"—low Dutch for tree. . . The most familiar appellation of her mother was "Mau-Mau Bett." She was the mother of some ten or twelve children. . . She was privileged to behold six of them while she remained a slave . . . [Isabella] wishes that all who would fain believe that slave parents have not natural affection for their offspring could have listened as she did, while Bomefree and Mau-Mau Bett. . .would sit for hours, recalling and recounting every endearing, as well as harrowing circumstance that taxed memory could supply, from the histories of those dear departed ones, of whom they had been robbed, and for whom their hearts still bled.

Mau-Mau Bett Remembers

Bomefree, I shall not be denied
the memory of my children.
Their touch, smell, smiles, yes
but not what I've stored
what I know without thinking on.
What is it, Bett?
That the Lord's mercy resides in Peter's brown eyes.
There's healing power in my young one's tears.
Only angels' songs rival the beauty of my girl's laughter.
They're gone, Bett. How can we know?
The last one, Isabella.
See how good He is, Bomefree?

"My children, there is a God, who hears and sees you."

"A God, Mau-Mau! Where does he live?" asked the children. "He lives in the sky," she replied, "and when you are beaten, or cruelly treated, or fall into any trouble, you must ask help of him and he will always hear and help you."

What I Learned of God

In the evening
under the heaven's sparkling vault
Mau-Mau called us
talked of God's mercy. I listened

carefully. Understood only
that God hears all
sees all. Expects praise
like a friendless beast devours fear.

Enough ails me
she'd say, bent in prayer
my siblings' recitation
always brief.

Years later I bowed beneath
lustrous night sky
faithful fear unwavering.

*I*n the evening, when her mother's work was done, she would sit down under the sparkling vault of heaven, and calling her children to her, would talk to them of the only Being that could effectually aid or protect them.

Mau-Mau Quilting

I remember Mau-Mau quilting
when day gave way
to whispers and fatigue
when the warmth of bodies in our small
home was just enough.
I followed her hands
read histories in each weft she wrote
as if crafting universal prayer.

One night I sat at the hem
the scroll cloth telling
a text no child could comprehend.

In from the fields
Bomefree treaded across
like an angry soldier
the quilt his battlefield
of shame and loss. I still recall
the dirt of his heel staining
one corner of my old calico dress.

At length, the never-to-be-forgotten day of the terrible auction arrived, when the "slaves, horses, and other cattle" of Charles Ardinburgh, deceased, were to be put under the hammer, and again change masters. Not only Isabella and Peter [her brother], but their mother, was now destined to the auction block. . .

Auction

One hundred dollars is just enough
to buy a slave girl, nine or ten years old.

She will not resist, bid high
higher, tell the world of your felony.

Watch her stand bare atop
warped planks, beneath warning signs.

How much for the one with the small eyes
pinch her firm flesh, tug at the nape.

Offer up currency for virgin blood
dream sacrifice to ward off obsession.

Blind and crippled, [Bomefree] was too superannuated to think for a moment of taking care of himself, and he greatly feared no persons would interest themselves in his behalf . . . While he was living this way, Isabella was twice permitted to visit him. Another time she walked twelve miles, and carried her infant in her arms to see him, but when she reached the place where she hoped to find him, he had just left for a place some twenty miles distant, and she never saw him more.

Bomefree's Last Testimony

They say freedom only come on paper
penned and declared. I say
it come like rain
when you need it most, when we can
no longer stand the drought
when too much life is taken.

Isabella never complained. Worked
hard as her brothers, birthed babies
to master's satisfaction. If she wanted love
I wouldn't know it.

Last time I saw her
there was thunder in her voice
the kind some tend to ignore
before the furious tide takes them.

*B*omefree. . .found his poor needs hardly supplied, as his new providers were scarce able to administer to their own wants. . .One day, an aged colored woman, named Soan, called at his shanty. . .he was suffering dreadfully with the filth and vermin that had collected upon him. . .Soan was herself an emancipated slave, old and weak. . .she lacked the courage to undertake a job of such seeming magnitude. . .and with great reluctance, and a heart swelling with pity. . .she felt obliged to leave him in his wretchedness and filth. And shortly after her visit, this faithful slave, this deserted wreck of humanity, was found on his miserable pallet, frozen and stiff in death.

Death of Bomefree

what becomes of a useless slave
when the casualties of labor warp the mind and gait
when the memory of lashings lingers in the flesh, sinew, bone
what happens to those used ones

beneath most any tree one finds fallen fruit
or leaves that quit the strapping branch
to loyal shorelines the ocean offers up shells
stilled but not silent

Bomefree waited
in a rude cabin
in a lone wood
blind and frozen
stiff in death
for friend or daughter
all used up and useless
but to his true Master

*D*uring the winter her feet were badly frozen, for want of proper covering. They gave [Isabella] plenty to eat, and also a plenty of whippings. One Sunday morning, in particular, she was told to go to the barn; on going there, she found her master with a bundle of rods, prepared in the embers, and bound together with cords. . .He whipped her till the flesh was deeply lacerated, and the blood streamed from her wounds—and the scars remain to the present day, to testify to the fact. . .In these hours of her extremity, she did forget the instructions of her mother, to go to God in all her trials, and every affliction. . .

In the Barn

One sudden morning he stormed about
anger streaming like sweat on a poor man's brow.
Twisting wrist, assaulting ear
he pinned me hard against the barn wall
as if for slaughter.

It was Sunday. The Lord awaited praise
but my soul was filled with survival. Still
I refused to scream out for my Master,
muted the mercy cry with each lashing.
Later under soft dark sky
I stared at palmflesh
now pierced from my own grip.
I clasped wet hands determined.

She had no idea God had any knowledge of her thoughts, save what she told him; or heard her prayers, unless they were spoken audibly. And consequently, she could not pray unless she had time and opportunity to go by herself, where she could talk to God without being overheard.

Faithful

From earthly doubt
I scaled the fragile scaffold.

Jesus approved but I
in disbelief
knew him not
only moved
by the tears and prayers
of others.

I stepped lightly toward
what I could not name
ambitious for the heavenprize.

Then glory
I stood with him
this known one
so much more than
my imagination could offer.

*M*rs. Dumont, who had been born and educated in a non-slaveholding family, and, like many others, used only to work-people, who, under the most stimulating of human motives, were willing to put forth their every energy, could not have patience with the creeping gait, the dull understanding, or see any cause for the listless manners and careless slovenly habits of the poor down-trodden outcast. . .

At the Stove

This morning steam ascends from bubbling pot
I close my eyes, spoon submerged, remember
a childhood dream. My eyes open, I see
fresh wounds on each hand, some caused in accident
others caught by surprise
all soothed by the warmth of broth.
How this old black skin glistens from lard and early sun.
Mrs. Dumont strolls through the kitchen
all she sees—
the good profit.

*A*s [Isabella] advanced in years, an attachment
sprung up between herself and a slave named
Robert. But his master, an Englishman by the name
of Catlin, anxious that no one's property but his
own should be enhanced by the increase of his slaves,
forbade Robert's visits to Isabella, and commanded
him to take a wife among his fellow-servants . . .

[O]ne Saturday afternoon, hearing that Bell was ill,
he took the liberty to go and see her . . . [Robert] made
his appearance; and the first people he met were his
old and his young masters . . . they both fell upon
him like tigers, beating him with the heavy ends of
their canes, bruising and mangling his head and face
in the most awful manner, and causing the blood,
which streamed from his wounds, to cover him like a
slaughtered beast . . . This beating, and we know not
what after treatment, completely subdued the spirit
of its victim, for Robert ventured no more to visit
Isabella, but like an obedient and faithful chattel,
took himself a wife from the house of his master.

Robert's Answer

I took a beating for Bell
not cause I loved her
or wanted to prove all that I whispered
in her ear each stolen night.

Sometimes the silence in her eyes
swallowed me like pride denied.
But I learned to tread up
return to stale Southern air
chance the distance from farm to farm
bear my sins in her ever welcome arms.

I went down that day
beneath white fists
to answer my Daddy years before
as he waited for death:
Will you be a man or a slave?

*A*nd if any one talked to [Isabella] of the injustice of her being a slave, she answered them with contempt, and immediately told her master. She then firmly believed that slavery was right and honorable. Yet she now sees very clearly the false position they were all in, both masters and slaves. . .

Her Sorrow

A slave woman I once knew
birthed seven children.
Named them all.
Sometimes we can hear her
calling each one
across fields, rivers, beyond
the daily wails, laughter
you can hear her.
Each name precise as air
Every now and then
an answer.

*I*n process of time, Isabella found herself the mother of five children, and she rejoiced in being permitted to be the instrument of increasing the property of her oppressors! Think, dear reader, without a blush, if you can, for one moment, of a mother thus willingly, and with pride, laying her own children, the "flesh of her flesh," on the altar of slavery. . .But we must remember that beings capable of such sacrifices are not mothers; they are only "things," "chattels," "property."

With Child at the Well

The morning of the day I bore
my fifth child I stood
at the edge of the well
peering.

Dark peace tempting
I thought I saw the face of my Lord
rippling like the fine, curious limbs
within me.

As I leaned in to soothe
my Savior's face
I stilled the blood
of my master
who knew not the wisdom of Jesus
but praised instead
the glory of profit.

After emancipation had been decreed by the State, some years before the time fixed for its consummation, Isabella's master told her if she would do well, and be faithful, he would give her "free papers," one year before she was legally free by statute. In the year 1826, she had a badly diseased hand, which greatly diminished her usefulness; but on the arrival of July 4, 1827, the time specified for her receiving her "free papers," [her master] refused granting it, on account (as he alleged) of the loss he had sustained by her hand. . .But Isabella inwardly determined that she would remain quietly with him only until she had spun his wool. . .and then she would leave him. . .

My Freedom

To say I ran away
would be untrue. I walked.

My freedom granted then denied
I bundled child, clothes, and fear
waited till dawn
then followed prayer's direction
each step confirming.

I gained the summit of a high hill
paused by my own courage
my grip lightened by fatigue
my faith reflected in the offensive sun.

That morning I became an answer to a question
my master never dare ask.

There was Charles Brodhead promised his slave Ned, that when harvesting was over, he might go and see his wife, who lived some twenty or thirty miles off. So Ned worked early and late, and as soon as the harvest was all in, he claimed the promised boon. His master said, he had merely told him he 'would see if he could go, when the harvest was over; but now he saw that he could not go.' But Ned, who still claimed a positive promise, on which he had fully depended, went on cleaning his shoes. His master asked him if he intended going, and on his replying 'yes,' took up a sled-stick that lay near him, and gave [Ned] such a blow on the head as broke his skull, killing him dead on the spot.

Alive

A tongue should not bear the memory of blood
the tangy sweetness of flesh torn
the ancestral river disturbed.

The old ones know
lashings sting like a searing cry ignored
but this is not a sound to rejoice.

Still, even I admit the subtle satisfaction
from the warm trickle
bruises reverberating like drums announcing
bloated skin the color of late summer plums

How tender we
the living
remain.

A little previous to Isabel's leaving her old master, he had sold her child, a boy of five years, to a Dr. Gedney, who took him with him as far as New York city, on his way to England; but finding the boy too small for his service, he sent him back to his brother, Solomon Gedney. This man disposed of him to his sister's husband, a wealthy planter, by the name of Fowler, who took him to his own home in Alabama. . .The law expressly prohibited the sale of any slave out of the State—and all minors were to be free at twenty-one years of age. . .When Isabel heard that her son had been sold South, she immediately started on foot and alone, to find the man who had thus dared, in the face of all law, human and divine, to sell her child out of the State; and if possible, to bring him to account for the deed.

Finding Peter

When they sold my Peter out of state
they broke their own laws.
Grand Jurors, legislators, constables all
servants of the Court
failed their own corruption
denied me a mother's pride.

The day I demanded his return
my words quivered
then grew big with contempt.
Each syllable gaining courage
my heartache relieved.

When the judge declared
me his only master
my Peter cast down his eyes
as did I.

*W*hen the pleading was at an end, Isabella understood the Judge to declare, as the sentence of the Court, that the "boy be delivered into the hands of the mother. . ." This sentence was obeyed; he was delivered into her hands, the boy meanwhile begging, most piteously, not to be taken from his dear master, saying she was not his mother, and that his mother did not live in such a place as that. . .[they succeeded] in convincing him that Isabella was not some terrible monster, as he had for the last months, probably, been trained to believe; and who, in taking him away from his master, was taking him from all good, and consigning him to all evil.

Peter's Lament

They say she is my mother
but what am I to do with a mother?
I have my fine master, the sea
and food. No need for motherlove.

Inside that house she waits
but how can I care for someone
who is worth less than my good shoes?

From ship to shore I have been
recaptured to surrender my birth
no currency to speak of
just inherited agony
pulling me to the ranks
I have grown to despise.

*T*hen a space seemed opening between her and God, and she felt that if some one, who was worthy in the sight of heaven, would but plead for her in their own name, and not let God know it came from her, who was so unworthy, God might grant it. At length, a friend appeared to stand between herself and an insulted Deity. . ."Who are you?" she exclaimed, as the vision brightened into a form distinct, beaming with the beauty of holiness, and radiant with love. "I know you—and I don't know you." At length, after bending both soul and body with the intensity of this desire. . .an answer came to her, saying distinctly, "It is Jesus." "Yes," she responded, "it is Jesus."

Friend

In the space between God and me
came Jesus. Light blossoming
fragrant dawn after
the turbulent eve. Familiar
as my previous condemnation.

This friend, this opened hand
led me to what I'd long forgotten
when Mau-Mau Bett whispered bedtime prayers
while round us skulked the shifting shadow:
Master outside the door, prowling
loud as the moon's glimmer.

Jesus, who stands beside me as I advance
toward God, once dreaded King
now my patient Prince.

How can I fear the shadow now?
Sweet peace my blessed protector.

*W*hile Isabella was in New York, her sister Sophia came from Newberg to reside in the former place. Isabella had been favored with occasional interviews with this sister, although at one time she lost sight of her for the space of seventeen years. . .and when she appeared before her again, handsomely dressed, she did not recognize her, till informed who she was. Sophia informed her that her brother Michael—a brother she had never seen—was in the city; and when she introduced him to Isabella, he informed her that their sister Nancy had been living in the city, and had deceased a few months before. . ."Oh, Lord," inquired Isabella, "what is this slavery, that it can do such dreadful things? What evil can it not do?"

A Sister's Dream

I'll see them again, brothers and sisters all.
Landscapes and laws can't replace
the memory of blood.

Yesterday the market was heavy
folks coming from ships, farms
moved by necessity and loneliness.
I sat on the edge of a warped crate
catching each passing eye, reading
lineage like quilt patterns.

If Belle passed, her eyes were most likely
heavencast.

*I*sabella's next decision was, that she must leave the city; it was no place for her; yea, she felt called in spirit to leave it, and to travel east and lecture. . .Having made what preparations she deemed necessary. . .about an hour before she left, she informed Mrs. Whiting, the woman of the house where she was stopping, that her name was no longer Isabella, but SOJOURNER; and that she was going east. And to her inquiry, "What are you going east for?" her answer was, "The Spirit calls me there, and I must go."

Landscape

Beyond that bend lies bountiful hope.
Sanctioned dangers lurk
but I will not be paused
by faith refused.

I keep pace on lonesome roads
stare down the cowardly pack
patrolling. Ghost men hide
watch me quickstep march
to hymnal jubilance.

Follow children, my journey
your inheritance.

Isabella was now fairly stated on her pilgrimage; her bundle in one hand, and a little basket of provisions in the other, and two York shillings in her purse—her heart strong in the faith that her true work lay before her, and that the Lord was her director. . .She walked on, the stars and the tiny horns of the new-moon shed but a dim light on her lonely way. . .

Testimony

I.

In the season of death
brown bodies fed white fear.

II.

In the clearing
a thin dark thing
still against the late
autumn breeze
the dangling form
a familiar posture
to those who dare roam
Southern back woods.
As I neared
the telling stench forewarned
beneath splendid sun
a bowed head
hands clasped
eyes testifying.

III.

I pray for good dreams
those that end with smiles, music
When I've worked all day
for my master
I ask only for nocturnal peace
to be like the moon
innocent of the sun's sins.

When she had convinced the people that she was a lover of God and his cause, and had gained a good standing with them, so that she could get a hearing among them, she had become quite sure in her own mind that they were laboring under a delusion, and she commenced to use her influence to calm the fears of the people, and pour oil upon the troubled waters.

Speak Speak

he said
and I did
and they listened
black white man woman
even child
      birds know
wicked winds from heavenbreath
guiding light their timely flight
      speak speak praise
beyond bruised hearts
sanctioned welts
on Christian land
life consumed
then denied
      children follow water
know the current
like a mother's blood
baptismal bound
      Darkness tempts
even loyal hearts
silenced by faithless
sacrifice
      glory abound
hear this deliverance song
      sing sing
      it won't be long

A *party of wild young men, with no motive but that of entertaining themselves by annoying and injuring the feelings of others, had assembled at the meeting, hooting and yelling, and in various ways interrupting the services. . .Sojourner. . .found herself quaking with fear. . .Under the impulse of this sudden emotion, she fled to the most retired corner of a tent, and secreted herself behind a trunk. . .she began to soliloquise as follows: "Shall I run away and hide from the Devil? Me, a servant of the living God? Have I not faith enough to go out and quell that mob, when I know it is written—"One shall chase a thousand, and two put ten thousand to flight?" . . . Sojourner left the tent alone and unaided, and walking some thirty rods to the top of a small rise of ground, commenced to sing. . .*

Battle

Sometimes I think my soul's a battleground
the fight that's become me charged by
trudging warriors careless for the cause.

I remind myself to welcome beauty, song, solace.
Just as blades of grass aim heavenbound
I preach toward the possibility of what I know.

Some nights I cry, giving ancestral blessing
to the babies and men and women I am charged to free.

Brethren, this is not a war of your flesh here today
like the splendid sunlight on your battered skin
but generations coming
should we survive the brutal blows.

Don't be alarmed if today I rest. My armor's
dulled but sturdy.

*I*n the spring of 1849, Sojourner made a visit to her eldest daughter, Diana, who has ever suffered from ill health, and remained with Mr. Dumont, Isabella's humane master. She found him still living, though advanced in age, and reduced in property. . .but greatly enlightened on the subject of slavery. He said he could then see that "slavery was the wickedest thing in the world, the greatest curse the earth had ever felt. . ." She received a letter from her daughter Diana, dated Hyde Park, December 19, 1849, which informed her that Mr. Dumont had "gone West" with some of his sons—that he had taken along with him, probably through mistake, the few articles of furniture she had left with him. . .She recalled the lectures he used to give his slaves, on speaking the truth and being honest, when he was stealing all the time himself, and did not know it! What a confession for a slavemaster to make to a slave!

To the Slave Master and His Confession

Steal the body, not the soul
and you are still guilty in the eyes of the Lord.
Law may absolve you
but not your heart
which beats with the blood of Jesus.

Discern your sins, prepare each one
before you go before the Lord. Make good
delayed promises, pay earthly debts
then pray for timely redemption.

Yours is not the only sin
this peculiar institution has wrought
Surely you are not alone
in the scandal,
mistresses and brethren alike must account.

But alone you'll stand
without jurisdiction, friend or slave to shield
the wrath designed by your own deeds.

Patience
your sole conciliation.

About the Author

Lita Hooper, Associate Professor of English at Georgia Perimeter College, earned an M.A. in Creative Writing from the University of Colorado and a D.A. in English and Humanities at Clark Atlanta University. She has produced and written for the stage, and her poetry has appeared in various publications. She is the author of the critical biography *Art of Work: The Life and Art of Haki Madhubuti* and co-editor of *44 on 44: Forty-Four African American Writers on the 44th President of the United States*. Hooper is a Cave Canem Fellow and an Emerging Artist Grant recipient of the City of Atlanta Office of Cultural Affairs.